Practice Tests for CASAS Math GOAL 2
Level D, Forms 927M and 928M

Helping Learners Develop Mathematical Thinking Skills, Approach Math with
Confidence, and Sharpen their Test-Taking Ability

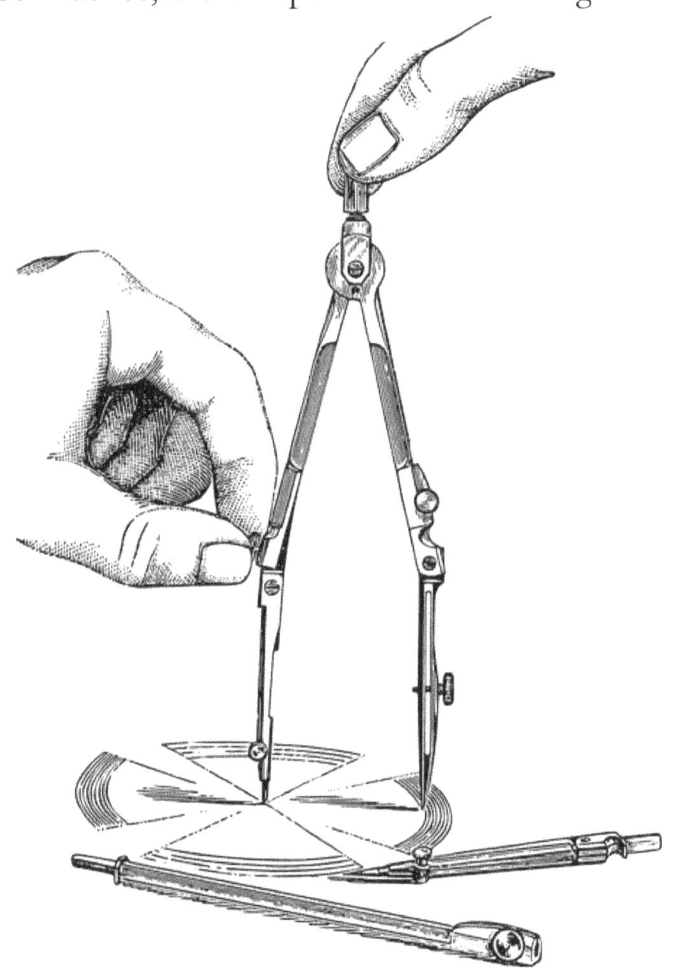

By

CBL | COACHING
FOR BETTER LEARNING

Copyright ©2024 Coaching for Better Learning, LLC

All rights reserved.

TABLE OF CONTENTS

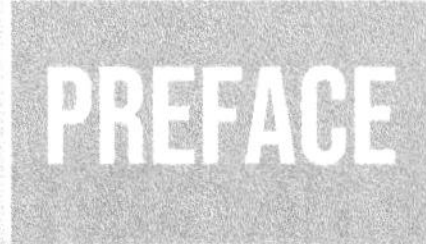

PREFACE

Dear Instructors,

This book entails four (4) practice tests and is designed to prepare adult learners for the CASAS Math GOALS 2, Level D Forms 927M and 928M. The practice tests align with the CASAS Competencies and meet the rigorous requirements of the College and Career Readiness Standards (CCRS), the National Reporting System (NRS), and the Workforce Innovation and Opportunity Act (WIOA).

Adhering to the CASAS Math GOALS 2 test blueprint, the practice tests assess learners' understanding of the following math areas: *Number Sense and Operations, Consumer Economics, Algebraic Thinking, Geometry, Data Analysis and Statistics, and Pure Mathematics.*

More importantly, this resource increases learners' confidence, guides them to reflect on their learning and progress, and helps them transfer their knowledge to other contexts. Each practice test includes real-world activities that promote deep understanding and practical application of mathematical concepts. An answer key also accompanies each test.

By using this resource, you can save time, distribute practice sessions over several weeks, and assess and reinforce your learners' understanding of math functions and concepts. To order class sets, visit cbledu.com.

The CBL Team,

Your Partner in Student Learning

INTRODUCTION

Dear Math Students,

This resource will help you develop and reinforce your math skills and test-taking ability. It will prepare you for the CASAS Math GOALS 2 Level D test. The practice tests will assess your understanding of the following math areas: *Number Sense and Operations, Consumer Economics, Algebraic Thinking, Geometry, Data Analysis and Statistics, and Pure Mathematics.*

Important Strategies:

Follow the strategies below to develop and reinforce your mathematical thinking skills and test-taking ability.

1. Study and master the four operations (addition, subtraction, multiplication, and division). Learn several strategies to compute and perform operations.

2. Study and master the multiplication table by reviewing it at least once daily (5 to 10 minutes).

3. Look up the meanings of math concepts (e.g., *sum, product, quotient, fraction, triangle*). Try to describe their meanings in your own words.

4. Seek to understand math ideas or the big picture before practicing the details or simple exercises. You can do that by using YouTube videos or Khan Academy.

5. Connect math ideas and concepts to real-world objects or situations. Ask your instructors for real-life examples.

6. Ask clarifying questions to ensure you understand everything before your class ends.

7. Practice solving word problems weekly (20-30 minutes) without distraction (TV, PC, cellphone, noise).

8. Solve math operations and problems on paper. Always show your work—including your strategies or reasoning—on paper.

9. Study and practice math in a group or with a classmate. Discuss your math solutions and strategies.

10. Explain math ideas and concepts to yourself or someone else orally. After doing this orally, you can also do it using drawings and writing.

11. Always reflect on your progress and strategies. After each practice session or test, identify what works well and why you make certain mistakes. Review and focus on practicing math ideas and concepts you don't understand well.

12. Celebrate your achievements. Any increase in math knowledge is an achievement.

Remember, math skills are essential for success in various aspects of your life, including community involvement, managing family finances, and professional advancement. By committing to completing the practice tests in this book, you'll be setting yourself up for success in your academic pursuits and beyond.

Let's get to work!

HOW TO APPROACH MATH WITH CONFIDENCE

Here are nine (9) practical ways you can overcome math fear and anxiety and build confidence while using this math book:

1. **Start Small:** Begin with easier problems that you can solve to build your confidence before solving harder ones.

2. **Use the book's Strategies:** Take advantage of this resource's strategies and practice tests. They are designed to help you understand, practice, and sharpen your math skills.

3. **Set Small Goals:** Break your math studies into small, achievable goals. Celebrate when you reach these goals to motivate yourself.

4. **Practice Regularly:** Consistent practice makes learning math more manageable. Try to work on math problems a few times a week.

5. **Take Breaks:** If you feel overwhelmed, take a short break. Come back to the math problems with a clear mind.

6. **Ask for Help:** Don't hesitate to seek help when you need it. Ask a teacher or a classmate, or use online resources if you're stuck.

7. **Stay Positive:** Keep a positive attitude about math. Remind yourself that you can handle it and that it's okay to make mistakes as you learn.

8. **Understand, Don't Memorize:** Focus on understanding the math ideas and concepts rather than just memorizing formulas. This understanding will make you feel more confident in solving math problems and taking math tests.

9. **Visualize Success:** Picture yourself successfully solving problems and understanding concepts. This visualization can boost your confidence.

By following these strategies, you will be able to study well and practice math with more confidence.

> Three teams played the Stock Market Game. They each started out with $21,000 to invest. The winning team is the one with the most money at the end. Team A made 3/5 more money, Team B made 65% more money, and Team C made a total of $31,970.

1. How much money did Team A make?

   A. $33,875

   B. $33,600

   C. $12,600

   D. $32,575

2. How much money did Team B make?

   A. $35,000

   B. $28,900

   C. $30,425

   D. $34,650

3. Which team won the game?

   A. Team B

   B. Team A

   C. Team C

4. Over time, the value of a car decreases. If the value of a car purchased for $37,500 decreased by 8.5% in a year, what would its value be at the end of the year?

   A. $31,200

   B. $29,750.25

   C. $34,312.50

   D. $33,500

> A cellular phone service is available for $35 per month for 500 minutes.

5. What is the monthly cost in dollars per minute?

   A. $1.15 per minute

   B. $0.05 per minute

   C. $0.07 per minute

   D. $0.08 per minute

6. What is the monthly cost in cents per minute?

A. 8 cents per minute

C. 0.08 cents per minute

B. 0.07 cents per minute

D. 7 cents per minute

7. How many feet per second are equivalent to 36 miles per hour?

A. 52.8 feet per second

C. 528 feet per second

B. 72 feet per second

D. 105.6 feet per second

8. Simplify the following expression:

$$\left(\frac{5^{17} \cdot 5^8}{5^{25}}\right)^{-1}$$

A. 1/5

C. 5

B. 1

D. 25

9. What is the value of x?

$$25\% \text{ of } x = 0.05x + 10$$

A. 25

C. 65

B. 40

D. 50

Look at the following receipt:

```
                STAPLE-STORE
              LOW PRICES, EVERY DAY
             2344, Staple Furniture Road
             Furniture City, CA, 211232

   SALE                      27981349442287755000
                             10/17/2020    17:23

   QTY          SKU                        PRICE

    1      HAND TOWEL
           023404213519                     2.97 N
    4      Office Chair
           069005841315                   359.56 N
    1      Office Table
           030424458834                   120.89 N
     SUBTOTAL                             $483.42
         Simple Tax  10.25%                $50.27
      TOTAL                                   ?

   CREDIT
   Card No  .:   xxxxxxxxxxxx 9999
   Chip Read
   Auth No  .: 688880
   AID  .: 6166TF6V3RC4
```

10. How many items were purchased?

    A. 3   C. 4

    B. 5   D. 6

11. What is the total amount?

    A. $533.69   C. $533.79

    B. $583.42   D. $522.89

12. What is the cost of a dozen office chairs?

    A. $4,314.72   C. $1078.68

    B. $1,121.07   D. $1,904.75

13. What is the cost of nine hand towels?

    A. $24.97   C. $31.68

    B. $26.73   D. $25.73

14. Mike walks 6.2 miles in 3/5 hours. What is the unit rate in miles per hour?

    A. 10.33 miles per hour   C. 12.30 miles per hour

    B. 9.33 miles per hour   D. 3.72 miles per hour

15. Tina can mow a lawn that measures 1,200 square feet in 2.5 hours. At that rate, how long would
    it take her to mow a lawn of 1,440 square feet?

    A. 4.5 hours   C. 3 hours

    B. 5 hours   D. 6.5 hours

> A bakery charges $3.75 for each cupcake and $4.00 for each brownie. Gina spent
> $54.50 purchasing 14 items at the bakery.

16. How many cupcakes did she purchase?

    A. 5   C. 7

    B. 8   D. 6

17. How many brownies did she purchase?

    A. 8   C. 7

    B. 10   D. 13

The population of foxes in a national park was 2,240 in 2014 and was recorded again to be 4,200 in 2018. Suppose that the population continues to grow linearly.

18. What is the rate change of this linear model?

    A. 375 foxes per year

    B. 350 foxes per year

    C. 490 foxes per year

    D. 390 foxes per year

19. Which linear function represents the fox population P, in terms of t, the years since 2014?

    A. P(t) = 390t + 2,240

    B. P(t) = 490t + 2,240

    C. P(t) = 490t + 4,200

    D. P(t) = 390t + 4,200

20. What is the fox population in 2025?

    A. 6,670 foxes

    B. 8,260 foxes

    C. 7,770 foxes

    D. 7,630 foxes

21. When will the population reach 12,040 foxes?

    A. Year 2034

    B. Year 2040

    C. Year 2039

    D. Year 2035

A rectangular tank has a length of 25 feet, a width of 12 feet, and a depth of 7 feet.

22. How many cubic feet of water can the tank hold?

    A. 1,880 ft^3

    B. 2,100 ft^3

    C. 2,000 ft^3

    D. 1,890 ft^3

23. The manufacturer suggests filling the tank to 90% capacity. How many cubic feet is this?

    A. 1,890 ft^3

    B. 1,990 ft^3

    C. 1,895 ft^3

    D. 2,000 ft^3

24. One cubic foot is approximately 7.48 gallons. How many gallons of water should be put in the tank at 90% capacity?

    A. 13,875.20 gal.

    B. 13,138.84 gal.

    C. 14,137.20 gal.

    D. 15,376.44 gal.

25. A box that is 21 inches wide, 32 inches high, and 5 inches thick is to be wrapped in gift paper. How many square inches of gift paper are needed?

A. 3,360 in^2

B. 1,874 in^2

C. 672 in^2

D. 1,965 in^2

26. A map scale indicates that 1/4 inch on the map corresponds with 6 real miles. How many miles apart are two cities that are 4 inches apart on the map?

A. 87 miles

B. 92 miles

C. 85 miles

D. 96 miles

27. A tree 36 feet tall casts a shadow 15 feet long. Mark is 6 feet tall. How long is Mark's shadow? (Hint: use similar triangles.)

A. 2.5 ft.

B. 3.3 ft.

C. 2.9 ft.

D. 3.5 ft.

28. Kevin runs 5 miles north and 6 miles west. What is the shortest distance he must travel to return to his starting point?

A. 11 miles

B. $\sqrt{11}$ miles

C. 8.7 miles

D. $\sqrt{61}$ miles

29. What is x?

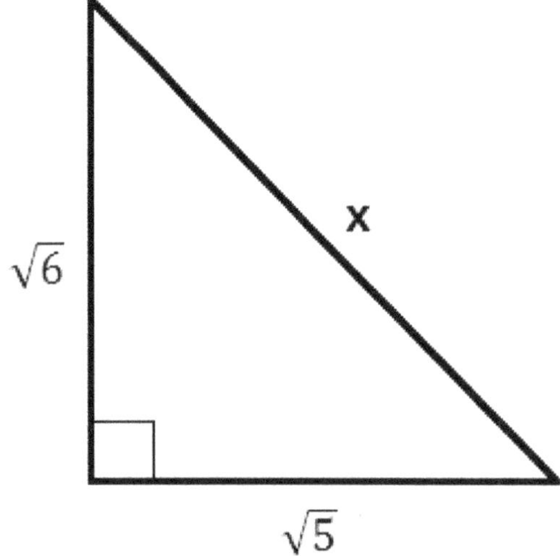

A. 11

B. $\sqrt{11}$

C. $\sqrt{6} + \sqrt{5}$

D. 13

The following table shows the number of survey subjects who have received and have not received speeding tickets in the last year, along with the color of their cars.

	Speeding ticket	No speeding ticket	Total
Black car	24	137	**A**
Blue car	58	318	**B**
Total	82	455	537

30. What is the value of A?

    A. 210

    B. 160

    C. 161

    D. 171

31. What is the value of B?

    A. 376

    B. 386

    C. 410

    D. 412

32. What is the probability that a randomly chosen person has a black car?

    A. 0.30

    B. 0.28

    C. 0.31

    D. 0.70

33. What is the probability that a randomly chosen person has a blue car?

    A. 0.31

    B. 0.85

    C. 0.82

    D. 0.70

34. What is the probability that a randomly chosen person has a blue car **and** got a speeding ticket?

    A. 0.15

    B. 0.08

    C. 0.11

    D. 0.14

35. The mean of the following data set is 6.4. What is x?

$$5.5, 7.5, x, 6.5, 8.5$$

    A. 3.5

    B. 4

    C. 5

    D. 4.5

36. A professor has recorded test grades for 25 students in his class, but one of the grades is no longer readable. If the mean score on the test is 82 and the mean of the 24 readable scores is 88, what is the value of the unreadable score?

A. 62

B. 45

C. 68

D. 75

Answer Key:

1) B	19) B
2) D	20) D
3) A	21) A
4) C	22) B
5) C	23) A
6) D	24) C
7) A	25) B
8) B	26) D
9) D	27) A
10) D	28) D
11) A	29) B
12) C	30) C
13) B	31) A
14) A	32) A
15) C	33) D
16) D	34) C
17) A	35) B
18) C	36) A

REFLECTION ON LEARNING

After completing Practice Test #1, reflect on your performance by answering the questions below. Discuss your responses with your instructor or a classmate.

1- What questions did you answer incorrectly? List the question numbers.

2- Review the list. What types of questions (operations, measurements, algebra, geometry, data analysis, statistics, graph, pie chart) did you answer incorrectly?

3- Review each question you've missed. Why do you think you answered the question incorrectly?

4- Based on the questions you missed, what math functions or concepts do you need to study and practice more? List them.

5- Review the question you got correctly. What strategies or methods did you use? What did you do well?

6- After reviewing all the questions, what questions do you have for your instructor?

You have 70 minutes to answer 36 questions.

1. Sheryl watched a turtle crawl 5.40 feet in one hour. The next hour, the turtle crawled 18/5 feet. How far did the turtle crawl in total?

   A. 8.5 ft.

   B. 9.3 ft.

   C. 10.2 ft.

   D. 9 ft.

2. Bob skated for 16 hours last week. This week, he skated 12.5% more. How long did he skate this week?

   A. 18.55 hours

   B. 18 hours

   C. 22.5 hours

   D. 24 hours

3. Out of 600 racers who started a marathon, 520 completed the race, 60 gave up, and 20 were disqualified. What percentage did not complete the marathon?

   A. 13.33%

   B. 16.33%

   C. 9.30%

   D. 11.75%

4. Susan ran 1,540 meters in 7 minutes and 30 seconds. What is the unit rate in meters per second?

   A. 4.4 meters per second

   B. 5.66 meters per second

   C. 3.42 meters per second

   D. 3.60 meters per second

5. A car is traveling at 100 miles per hour. How far does it travel in 45 seconds?

   A. 3.5 miles

   B. 8.5 miles

   C. 1.25 miles

   D. 10.5 miles

6. 75 % of 3x is equal to 270. What is x?

   A. 80

   B. 150

   C. 360

   D. 120

7. Compute

$$\frac{\sqrt{81} + \sqrt{121} + \sqrt{225}}{\sqrt[3]{1}}$$

A. 29

C. 33

B. 35

D. 18

8. Simplify the following expression:

$$\frac{(6^3 \cdot 6^2)^2}{(6^6)^0}$$

A. 216

C. 6^{10}

B. 6^4

D. 6^{16}

Look at the following gas station receipt:

```
Passmore Gas & Propane
FG62326873455
3685 Charles Street
Livonia, MT
81065

9/12/2018   576646188
11:54 AM

XXXXXXXXXXXX2323
visa
INVOICE 831332
AUTH 138864

PUMP#24
Regular                19.56G
PRICE/GAL              $2.98

FUEL TOTAL               .?

    -----------
    Total  =             ?
CREDIT
============================
```

9. What is the price of a gallon of gas?

A. $3.55

C. $19.58

B. $2.98

D. $4.27

10. What is the total amount?

A. $56.66

C. $58.35

B. $58.74

D. $60.12

11. What is the cost of 40 gallons of gas?

    A. $105.00   C. $119.20

    B. $96.90   D. $179.99

12. Rebecca walks 4.75 miles in 1.20 hours. What is the unit rate in miles per hour?

    A. 4.18 miles per hour   C. 3.52 miles per hour

    B. 3.15 miles per hour   D. 3.96 miles per hour

13. A truck can hold 3,500 gallons of water. The truck can deliver 300 gallons of water every three minutes. How long will it take for the truck to empty the tank?

    A. 55 minutes   C. 35 minutes

    B. 32 minutes   D. 44 minutes

14. Solve the following pair of simultaneous linear equations:

$$A + B = 343$$

$$A - B = 87$$

    A. $A = 215, B = 128$ C. $A = 300, B = 43$

    B. $A = 128, B = 215$ D. $A = 250, B = 93$

15. Jodie wrote the following algebraic expression: **$7x - 0.20x$**. What would be the phrase that represents the algebraic expression?

    A. Seven minus the product of 0.20 and a number

    C. The difference between seven times a number and 0.20

    B. Seven times a number minus 0.20

    D. The difference between seven times a number and 20% of the number

A company sells smart TVs. They incur a fixed cost of $23,800 for rent, insurance, and other expenses. It costs $170 to produce each smart TV. Let x be the number of smart TVs produced.

16. What is the linear function that represents the company's cost, C, as a function of x?

    A. $C(x) = 170 + 23,800x$ C. $C(x) = 23,800 - 170x$

    B. $C(x) = 23,800 + 170x$ D. $C(x) = (23,800 + 170)x$

17. What is the cost of producing 2,000 smart TVs?

   A. $363,800

   B. $380,800

   C. $372,500

   D. $373,800

18. If the company does not produce a single smart TV, what is the total cost?

   A. $25,500

   B. $23,970

   C. $23,000

   D. $23,800

19. To complete a job, five workers get paid at the rate of $18.50 per hour. If the total payment for the job was $647.50, how many hours did the five workers spend on the job?

   A. 7 hours

   B. 8.5 hours

   C. 6 hours

   D. 9.5 hours

20. Which shape has the most corners?

   A. Sphere

   B. Hexagon

   C. Right triangle

   D. Trapezoid

21. Which of the following is true?

   A. The volume of a rectangle is more than 0.

   B. The surface area of a sphere is measured in cubic feet.

   C. A cylinder has no corners.

   D. Congruent figures have different sizes.

22. The surface area of a cube is 486 square feet. What is the volume of the cube?

   A. 81 ft^3

   B. 243 ft^3

   C. 512 ft^3

   D. 729 ft^3

23. A cylinder with a base radius of 12 inches and a height of 16 inches is to be wrapped in gift paper. How many square inches of gift paper are needed? (use $\pi = 3.14$)

   A. 7,234 in^2

   B. 4,220.16 in^2

   C. 2,156.55 in^2

   D. 2,110.08 in^2

24. A map scale indicates that x inch on the map corresponds with 8 real miles. Two towns that are 22.5 inches apart on the map represent 60 real miles. What is x?

   A. 3

   B. 3.8

   C. 5

   D. 4.75

25. If the scale factor is 3/5, then the size of the new shape is

A. The same.

B. Enlarged.

C. Reduced.

D. None of the above.

26. Benny drives 9 miles south and 40 miles east. What is the shortest distance he must travel to return to his starting point?

A. 41 miles

B. $\sqrt{49}$ miles

C. 49 miles

D. $\sqrt{31}$ miles

27. What is x?

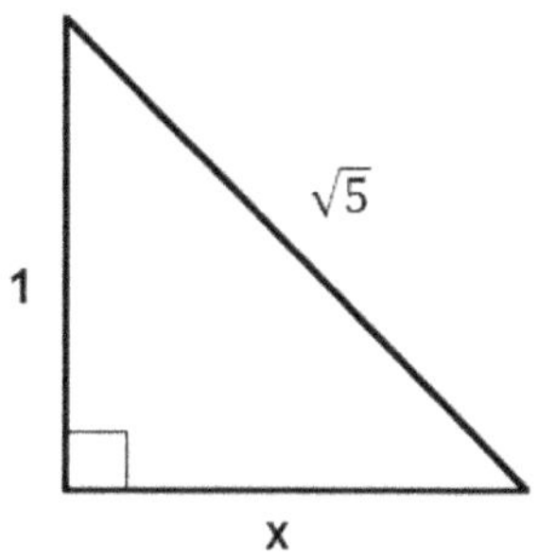

A. 4

B. $\sqrt{3}$

C. $\sqrt{5}-1$

D. 2

Several people were tested for two diseases. The following table shows the results:

	Positive Test	Negative Test	Total
Disease 1	13	21	34
Disease 2	**B**	344	**A**
Total	**C**	365	430

28. What is the value of A?

A. 311

B. 396

C. 281

D. 170

29. What is the value of B?

A. 52

B. 47

C. 51

D. 50

30. What is the value of C?

    A. 67   C. 65

    B. 68   D. 50

31. What is the probability that a random person does not have Disease 2?

    A. 91.10%   C. 81.33%

    B. 97.85%   D. 92.10%

32. What is the probability that a random person got a positive test?

    A. 11.27%   C. 28.97%

    B. 15.11%   D. 14.56%

33. The mean of the following data set is 14.25. What is x?

$$14, 14, 14, 14, 14, x, 14, 14$$

    A. 14   C. 18

    B. 16   D. 15

> The following data set shows scores on a math test:
> 84, 45, 71, 87, 85, 78, 77, 81, 77

34. What is the mean of the data set?

    A. 75.44   C. 81.20

    B. 76.11   D. 78

35. What is the median of the data set?

    A. 85   C. 77

    B. 87   D. 78

36. What is the outlier in the data set, if one exists?

    A. 45   C. 71

    B. 84   D. There is no outlier.

1) D	19) A
2) B	20) B
3) A	21) C
4) C	22) D
5) C	23) D
6) D	24) A
7) B	25) C
8) C	26) A
9) B	27) D
10) C	28) B
11) C	29) A
12) D	30) C
13) C	31) D
14) A	32) B
15) D	33) B
16) B	34) B
17) A	35) D
18) D	36) A

REFLECTION ON LEARNING

After completing Practice Test #2, reflect on your performance by answering the questions below. Discuss your responses with your instructor or a classmate.

1- What questions did you answer incorrectly? List the question numbers.

2- Review the list. What types of questions (operations, measurements, algebra, geometry, data analysis, statistics, graph, pie chart) did you answer incorrectly?

3- Review each question you've missed. Why do you think you answered the question incorrectly?

4- Based on the questions you missed, what math functions or concepts do you need to study and practice more? List them.

5- Review the question you got correctly. What strategies or methods did you use? What did you do well?

6- After reviewing all the questions, what questions do you have for your instructor?

You have 70 minutes to answer 36 questions.

1. Rick wants to make 180 birdhouses. He can make 5 birdhouses per day. He has already made 45. How many days will it take him to get to 180 birdhouses?

   A. 25

   B. 18

   C. 27

   D. 24

2. Kenny has $4,236. Pam has five times more money than Kenny. How much money does Pam have?

   A. $25,300

   B. $28,633

   C. $22,190

   D. $21,180

3. There are 355 bears in Park A. There are nine times as many bears in Park B. Which expression will help us find out how many bears there are in Park B?

   A. $355 + 9$

   B. 9×355

   C. $355 - 9$

   D. $355 \div 9$

4. Charlie filled a bucket with 6 gallons of paint. Later, he poured out 3/4 of a gallon of the paint. How much paint is left in the bucket?

   A. 5.25 gal.

   B. 6.15 gal.

   C. 5.75 gal.

   D. 5.50 gal.

5. Compute

$$1.75 \times \left(\frac{5}{8} - \frac{1}{8}\right)$$

   A. 0.875

   B. 0.55

   C. 0.615

   D. 0.218

6. Which of the following expresses 14/25 as a percentage?

   A. 62%

   B. 54%

   C. 45%

   D. 56%

7. Which of the following expresses 1.23 as a percentage?

    A. 1.23%   C. 123%

    B. 12.3%   D. 0.123%

8. What is 120% of 120?

    A. 152   C. 144

    B. 148   D. 137

9. Compute

$$\left(\sqrt{36} + \sqrt{100} + \sqrt{169}\right)^2$$

    A. 29   C. 116

    B. 58   D. 841

10. What is n?

$$(2^4)^{\,6} = 2^{20+n}$$

    A. 4   C. 2^{12}

    B. 2^4 D. 2

11. Which of the following is the greatest?

    A. $5^4 \times 5$ C. $\sqrt{625}$

    B. 5^{-5} D. $(5^5)^{\,2}$

12. Daniel can run 9/2 miles in 1/4 hour. What is the unit rate in miles per hour?

    A. 16 mph.   C. 15.75 mph.

    B. 18 mph.   D. 20.5 mph.

13. Peter paid $44.40 for a dozen cans of beans. What is the unit rate in dollars per can?

    A. $3.7 per can   C. $3.5 per can

    B. $4.6 per can   D. $3.9 per can

> A cyclist rides his bike at a rate of 36
> miles per hour.

14. What is this rate in miles per minute?

A. 0.4 miles per minute

C. 0.6 miles per minute

B. 1.2 miles per minute

D. 0.8 miles per minute

15. What is this rate in miles per second?

A. 0.01 miles per second

C. 0.9 miles per second

B. 0.05 miles per second

D. 0.02 miles per second

16. How many miles will the cyclist travel in 25 minutes?

A. 12 miles

C. 20 miles

B. 18 miles

D. 15 miles

17. How many miles will the cyclist travel in 40 seconds?

A. 0.04 miles

C. 4 miles

B. 0.4 miles

D. 0.2 miles

> The linear function $d(t) = 450t + 6{,}120$ can be used to approximate the total average credit card debt in a U.S. household (in dollars) t years after 2000.

18. What is the rate of change of this linear model?

A. $6,120

C. $6,120 per year

B. $450 per year

D. $450

19. What is the total average credit card debt in the year 2013?

A. $11, 970

C. $21,840

B. $20,700

D. $20,070

20. In the year 2031, the total average credit card debt will be:

A. $11,970

C. $11,880

B. $10,780

D. $20,070

> The radius of the base of a cylindrical tank is 15 feet and the height is 18 feet.

21. How many cubic feet of water can the tank hold?

A. 3,108 ft^3 C. 12,717 ft^3

B. 12,100 ft^3 D. 11,790 ft^3

22. The manufacturer suggests filling the tank to 88% capacity. How many cubic feet is this?

A. 11,550.79 ft^3 C. 12,325.7 ft^3

B. 11,990.8 ft^3 D. 11,190.96 ft^3

23. What is the surface area of the tank?

A. 3,108 ft^2 C. 3,207 ft^2

B. 2,170 ft^2 D. 3,710 ft^2

24. What is the area of the following shape?

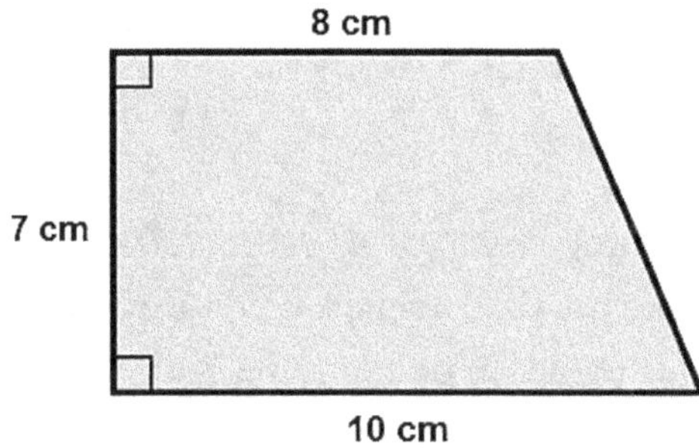

A. 126 cm^2 C. 74 cm^2

B. 25 cm^2 D. 63 cm^2

25. Two legs of a right triangle measure 4 inches and 7 inches. What is the length of the hypotenuse?

A. 11   C. $\sqrt{65}$

B. $\sqrt{11}$ D. 13

26. What is the length of the diagonal MN of the following rectangle?

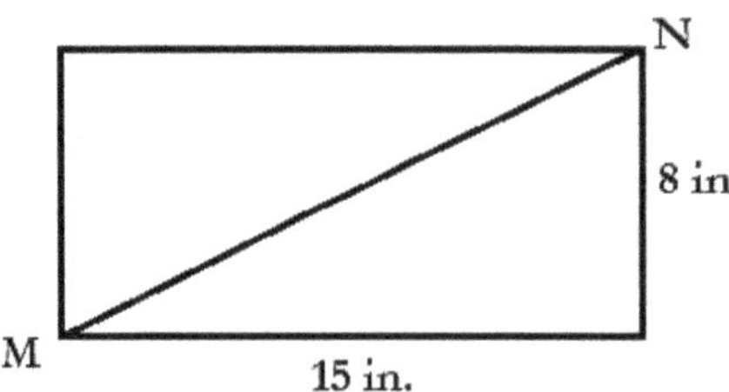

A. 23 in.   C. $\sqrt{23}$ in.

B. 17 in.   D. $\sqrt{161}$ in.

27. A miniature model of a building is made using the scale 3 inches = 18 feet. If the height of the building is 45 feet, what is the height of the miniature model?

A. 7.5 in.   C. 7.2 in.

B. 8 in.   D. 6.6 in.

The following two-way table shows some information about the number of items a factory makes in one month.

	Small	Medium	Large	Total
Item A	44	86	61	191
Item B	72	**B**	24	**A**
Item C	66	34	28	128
Total	182	**C**	113	470

28. What is A?

A. 133   C. 151

B. 141   D. 183

29. What is B?

A. 52   C. 47

B. 55   D. 51

30. What is C?

A. 175   C. 171

B. 155   D. 173

31. What is the total number of Item B made in a month?

A. 55   C. 151

B. 470   D. 159

32. What percentage of Item C was made in a month?

    A. 28.5%   C. 37.23%

    B. 27.23%   D. 28.9%

33. What is the probability of getting a number less than 5 when a die is rolled?

    A. 1/3   C. 1/6

    B. 1/2   D. 2/3

The following data set shows the number of points scored by a basketball team over its last 10 games:

77, 81, 70, 66, 88, 92, 90, 77, 94, 69

34. What is the mean of the data set?

    A. 80.4   C. 80

    B. 81   D. 82.6

35. What is the median of the data set?

    A. 92   C. 79

    B. 88   D. 90

36. What is the mode of the data set?

    A. 69   C. 81

    B. 77   D. There is no mode.

Answer Key:

1) C	19) A
2) D	20) D
3) B	21) C
4) A	22) D
5) A	23) A
6) D	24) D
7) C	25) C
8) C	26) B
9) D	27) A
10) A	28) C
11) D	29) B
12) B	30) A
13) A	31) C
14) C	32) B
15) A	33) D
16) D	34) A
17) B	35) C
18) D	36) B

REFLECTION ON LEARNING

After completing Practice Test #3, reflect on your performance by answering the questions below. Discuss your responses with your instructor or a classmate.

1- What questions did you answer incorrectly? List the question numbers.

2- Review the list. What types of questions (operations, measurements, algebra, geometry, data analysis, statistics, graph, pie chart) did you answer incorrectly?

3- Review each question you've missed. Why do you think you answered the question incorrectly?

4- Based on the questions you missed, what math functions or concepts do you need to study and practice more? List them.

5- Review the question you got correctly. What strategies or methods did you use? What did you do well?

6- After reviewing all the questions, what questions do you have for your instructor?

PRACTICE TEST #4

1. There are 2,875 pieces in a jigsaw puzzle. How many pieces are there in 14 puzzles?

   A. 40,250

   B. 39,520

   C. 40,205

   D. 39,995

2. If Jamal runs 2.45 miles every day, how many miles does he run in three weeks?

   A. 7.35 mi.

   B. 25.67 mi.

   C. 51.45 mi.

   D. 17.15 mi.

3. Laurie used 5/2 bags of apples to make five pies. How many bags of apples did she use for each pie?

   A. 2

   B. 1/2

   C. 2.5

   D. 3

4. Dan bought iron tubes that are each 2.25 feet long. If he makes a line of 18 tubes by placing them end-to-end, how long will it be?

   A. 45 ft.

   B. 40.5 ft.

   C. 41.25 ft.

   D. 41.1 ft.

5. Which of the following is equivalent to 24%?

   A. 1/15

   B. 7/20

   C. 8/15

   D. 6/25

6. Which of the following expresses 9/5 as a percentage?

   A. 80%

   B. 95%

   C. 145%

   D. 180%

7. A car can travel 420 miles on a full tank of gas. A more efficient car can travel 18% farther. How many miles farther can it travel on a full tank?

   A. 75.6 mi.

   B. 98 mi.

   C. 66.6 mi.

   D. 50 mi.

8. What is 150% of 2?

   A. 30   C. 3

   B. 6   D. 1.5

9. What is k?

$$\sqrt{k} = 14$$

   A. 28   C. 56

   B. 196   D. 184

10. What is m?

$$(3^m)^3 = 3^{27}$$

   A. 24   C. 6

   B. 12   D. 9

11. Emma can make 15 pairs of earrings in one week. Assuming she works at this constant rate, how many complete pairs of earrings can she make in 28 days?

   A. 60 pairs   C. 43 pairs

   B. 56 pairs   D. 65 pairs

12. A person types 150 words in 2 minutes. How much time does he take to type 1,350 words?

   A. 16 minutes   C. 22 minutes

   B. 18 minutes   D. 20 minutes

> A cyclist rides his bike at a rate of 24 miles per hour.

13. What is this rate in miles per minute?

   A. 0.4 miles per minute   C. 0.6 miles per minute

   B. 0.5 miles per minute   D. 0.9 miles per minute

14. If 1 mile = 5,280 feet, what is this rate in feet per second?

   A. 36 feet per second   C. 34.6 feet per second

   B. 28.5 feet per second   D. 35.2 feet per second

15. How many feet will the cyclist travel in 35 seconds?

    A. 1,225 feet   C. 1,120 feet

    B. 1,232 feet   D. 1,275 feet

16. How many miles will the cyclist travel in 4.5 hours?

    A. 110 miles   C. 108 miles

    B. 121 miles   D. 116 miles

> Nick is selling ice cream at the local fair. He is paid a fixed amount of $570 plus $0.85 per item sold. The equation that represents this situation is $P(n) = 0.85n + 570$, where P is the amount he is paid for the week and n is the number of ice cream he sold.

17. What is the rate of change of this linear model?

    A. $570   C. $0.85 per item

    B. $570 per item   D. $0.85

18. How much will Nick be paid if he sells 260 ice creams?

    A. $805   C. $800

    B. $793   D. $791

19. How many ice creams did Nick sell if he earned $923.60?

    A. 416   C. 421

    B. 522   D. 511

20. A store charges 12.5% more than what they pay for their merchandise. Which expression can be used to calculate what they should charge the customers?

    A. 12.5x   C. 1.25x

    B. x + 12.5   D. 1.125x

21. On a math exam, the highest grade was 33 points higher than the lowest grade. The sum of the two grades was 151. What was the highest grade?

    A. 87   C. 94

    B. 92   D. 59

22. What is the solution of the following equation?

$$12x - 12 = 12$$

A. $x = 4$

C. $x = 1$

B. $x = 2$

D. $x = 3$

23. What is the area of the following shape? (Use $\pi = 3.14$)

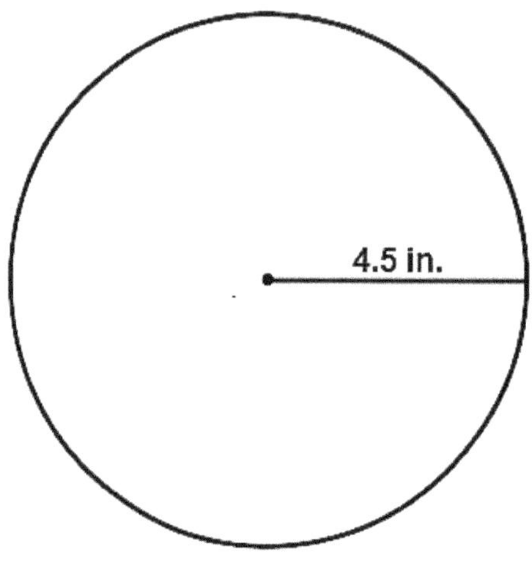

A. 28.26 in^2

C. 63.59 in^2

B. 65.73 in^2

D. 63.88 in^2

24. What is the height that we can reach with a 10 feet ladder leaning against a wall if the bottom of the ladder is 6 feet from the wall?

A. 7 ft.

C. 16 ft.

B. $\sqrt{136}$ ft.

D. 8 ft.

25. The following figure is formed by a square and a right triangle. What is the area of the square?

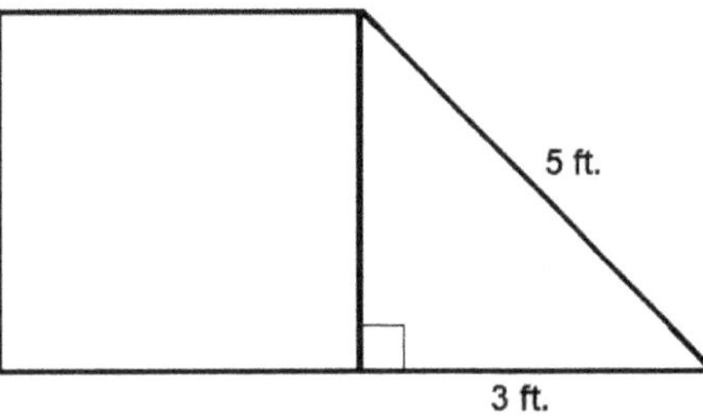

A. 16 ft²   C. 18 ft²

B. 4 ft²   D. 8 ft²

26. Jack drew Sandra in his sketchbook using a scale of 3 inches = 5 feet. If Sandra is 6 feet tall, how tall is she in the drawing?

A. 4.5 in.   C. 5.2 in.

B. 2.7 in.   D. 3.6 in.

The following two-way frequency table shows the preference for cats or dogs in two clubs:

Preference	Club A	Club B	Total
Prefer cats	16	**A**	51
Prefer dogs	27	18	45
No preference	7	8	15
Total	50	**B**	**C**

27. What is A?

A. 33   C. 31

B. 35   D. 42

28. What is B?

A. 58   C. 67

B. 61   D. 51

29. What is C?

    A. 111

    B. 115

    C. 101

    D. 93

30. What percentage prefers dogs?

    A. 41.55%

    B. 37.93%

    C. 40.54%

    D. 38.94%

31. What is the probability of getting a number more than 6 when a die is rolled?

    A. 1/6

    B. 1/3

    C. 1/4

    D. 0

32. A spinner has five equal sectors colored blue, green, red, orange, and yellow. What is the probability of landing on green after spinning it?

    A. 20%

    B. 25%

    C. 15%

    D. 30%

33. A number from 1 to 18 is chosen at random. What is the probability of choosing an even number?

    A. 25%

    B. 45%

    C. 54%

    D. 50%

34. What is the value that occurs most often of a given data set?

    A. Median

    B. Outlier

    C. Mode

    D. Mean

35. The mean of the following data set is 4.9. What is x?

$$4.2, 5.3, 6.6, x, 7.7, 2.5$$

    A. 4.8

    B. 3.1

    C. 3.8

    D. 2.9

36. What is the median of the following data set?

$$100, 90, 80, 100, 100, 80, 70, 90$$

    A. 90

    B. 95

    C. 100

    D. 85

1) A	19) A
2) C	20) D
3) B	21) B
4) B	22) B
5) D	23) C
6) D	24) D
7) A	25) A
8) C	26) D
9) B	27) B
10) D	28) B
11) A	29) A
12) B	30) C
13) A	31) D
14) D	32) A
15) B	33) D
16) C	34) C
17) C	35) B
18) D	36) A

REFLECTION ON LEARNING

After completing Practice Test #4, reflect on your performance by answering the questions below. Discuss your responses with your instructor or a classmate.

1- What questions did you answer incorrectly? List the question numbers.

2- Review the list. What types of questions (operations, measurements, algebra, geometry, data analysis, statistics, graph, pie chart) did you answer incorrectly?

3- Review each question you've missed. Why do you think you answered the question incorrectly?

4- Based on the questions you missed, what math functions or concepts do you need to study and practice more? List them.

5- Review the question you got correctly. What strategies or methods did you use? What did you do well?

6- After reviewing all the questions, what questions do you have for your instructor?

CBL
COACHING
FOR BETTER LEARNING

CASAS
TEST PREP
STUDENT
BOOK
FOR
MATH GOALS FORM
913 M LEVEL A/B

CASAS
TEST PREP
STUDENT
BOOK
FOR
MATH GOALS FORM
914 M LEVEL A/B
Preparing Adult Students for CASAS Math GOALS Tests
and for Workforce Entrance Math Exams
By Coaching for Better Learning, LLC

CASAS
TEST PREP
STUDENT
BOOK
FOR
MATH GOALS FORM
917 M LEVEL C/D
Preparing Adult Students for CASAS Math GOALS Tests
and for Workforce Entrance Math Exams
By Coaching for Better Learning, LLC

CASAS
TEST PREP
STUDENT
BOOK
FOR
MATH GOALS FORM
918 M LEVEL C/D

CASAS
TEST PREP
STUDENT
BOOK
READING GOALS
FORM 901R/902R

CASAS
TEST PREP
STUDENT
BOOK
FOR
READING GOALS
FORM 903R/904R
LEVEL B

CASAS
TEST PREP
STUDENT
BOOK
FOR
READING GOALS
LEVEL C
Preparing Adult Learners for CASAS
Reading GOALS Tests and for Workforce
and College Reading
By Coaching for Better Learning, LLC

CASAS
TEST PREP
STUDENT
BOOK
FOR
READING GOALS
FORM 907R/908R
LEVEL D
Preparing Adult Learners for CASAS
Reading GOALS Tests and for Workforce
and College Reading
By Coaching for Better Learning, LLC

TEST PREP MATH BOOK
FOR
CASAS Math GOALS 2
Level B—Forms 923M and 924M
CBL COACHING
FOR BETTER LEARNING

TEST PREP MATH BOOK
FOR
CASAS Math GOALS 2
Level E—Forms 929M and 930M
CBL COACHING
FOR BETTER LEARNING

TEST PREP MATH BOOK
FOR
CASAS Math GOALS 2
Level D—Forms 925M and 926M
CBL COACHING
FOR BETTER LEARNING

Test Prep Reading Book
for
CASAS Reading STEPS
Level B—Forms 623R & 624R
CBL

Test Prep Reading Book
for
CASAS Reading STEPS
Level C—Forms 625R & 626R
CBL

LEARNING
& STUDY GUIDE
FOR ADULT STUDENTS
A Must-Have Guide for Adult Ed Instructors
Bundle: Student Guide & Teacher's Manual
CBL COACHING
FOR BETTER LEARNING
By Coaching for Better Learning, LLC

LEARNING
& STUDY GUIDE
FOR ADULT STUDENTS
A Must-Have Guide for Adult Students
CBL COACHING
FOR BETTER LEARNING
By Coaching for Better Learning, LLC

TABE
11 & 12
STUDENT MATH MANUAL
AND PRACTICE TESTS
FOR LEVEL A
Preparing Adult Learners
to Ace TABE 11 & 12 Math Test Level A
By Coaching for Better Learning, LLC

TABE
11 & 12
STUDENT MATH MANUAL
AND PRACTICE TESTS
FOR LEVEL D
Preparing Adult Learners
to Ace TABE 11 & 12 Math Test Level D
By Coaching for Better Learning, LLC

TABE
11 & 12
STUDENT MATH MANUAL
AND PRACTICE TESTS
FOR LEVEL E
Preparing Adult Learners
to Ace TABE 11 & 12 Math Test Level E
By Coaching for Better Learning, LLC

TABE
11 & 12
STUDENT MATH MANUAL
AND PRACTICE TESTS
FOR LEVEL M
Preparing Adult Learners
to Ace TABE 11 & 12 Math Test Level M
By Coaching for Better Learning, LLC

GED
Math Study
Guide
FOCUSING ON
MATHEMATICAL REASONING
AND THINKING
By Coaching for Better Learning, LLC

ADULT ED
MATH
NUMBER SYSTEM, NUMBER SENSE, AND OPERATIONS PREPARING
FOR
CASAS, TABE 11 & 12, HISET, AND GED TESTING
BY COACHING FOR BETTER LEARNING

ADULT ED
MATH
GEOMETRY PREPARING
FOR
CASAS, TABE 11 & 12, HISET, AND GED TESTING
BY COACHING FOR BETTER LEARNING

CBL COACHING
Math
Practice Worksheets and Workbook for Adult Students
A learner-centered tool designed to help students practice and master the four operations while preparing them for CASAS Math GOALS 2, TABE 11 and 12, ACY, HISET, GED tests, and IET programs.

SKILLS FOR SUCCESS
IN CAREER AND
TECHNICAL EDUCATION (CTE)
STUDENT GUIDE
A SYSTEMATIC WAY TO MASTER ORGANIZATIONAL AND SOFT SKILLS
CBL COACHING

HOW TO ACHIEVE BETTER STUDENT RETENTION IN ADULT EDUCATION
Secrets to becoming an indispensable adult-ed teacher that provides a learning experience that's hard to walk away from (and keeps administrators happy!)
TEDDY EDOUARD

TABE 11 & 12 CONSUMABLE STUDENT READING MANUAL FOR LEVEL E
Preparing Adult Learners for TABE 11 & 12 Reading Tests and for Vocational Training and College Entrance Reading Exams
By Coaching for Better Learning, LLC

TABE 11 & 12 CONSUMABLE STUDENT READING MANUAL FOR LEVEL M
Preparing Adult Learners for TABE 11 & 12 Reading Tests and for Vocational Training and College Entrance Reading Exams
By Coaching for Better Learning, LLC

TABE 11 & 12 CONSUMABLE STUDENT READING MANUAL FOR LEVEL D
Preparing Adult Learners for TABE 11 & 12 Reading Tests and for Vocational Training and College Entrance Reading Exams
By Coaching for Better Learning, LLC

TABE 11 & 12 STUDENT LANGUAGE MANUAL FOR LEVEL E
Preparing Adult Learners for TABE 11 & 12 Language Tests and for Vocational Training and College Entrance Exams
By Coaching for Better Learning, LLC

TABE 11 & 12 STUDENT LANGUAGE MANUAL FOR LEVEL M
Preparing Adult Learners for TABE 11 & 12 Language Tests and for Vocational Training and College Entrance Exams
By Coaching for Better Learning, LLC

Preparing Adult Learners for TABE 11 & 12 Math Tests and for Vocational Training Entrance Math Exams
TABE 11 & 12 Consumable Student Math Workbook
FOR LEVEL E
By Coaching for Better Learning, LLC

Preparing Adult Learners for TABE 11 & 12 Math Tests and for Vocational Training Entrance Math Exams
TABE 11 & 12 Consumable Student Math Workbook
FOR LEVEL M
By Coaching for Better Learning, LLC

Preparing Adult Learners for TABE 11 & 12 Math Tests and for Vocational Training Entrance Math Exams
TABE 11 & 12 Consumable Student Math Workbook
FOR LEVEL D
By Coaching for Better Learning, LLC

Preparing Adult Learners for TABE 11 & 12 Math Tests and for Vocational Training Entrance Math Exams
TABE 11 & 12 Consumable Student Math Workbook
FOR LEVEL A
By Coaching for Better Learning, LLC

CBL COACHING
Workbook
Number and Letter Tracing for Adult Students
This tool is designed to help adult students practice and master handwriting. It is appropriate for literacy, ESL, and ABE classes.

READING NOTEBOOK & JOURNAL
For Adult Students
By Coaching For Better Learning   CBL COACHING

MATH NOTEBOOK & JOURNAL
For Adult Students
By Coaching For Better Learning   CBL COACHING

BOOK 1
PHONICS AND LIFE SKILLS READING
FOR
Adult Literacy, ABE, and ESL Students
Turning Learners into Proficient Readers
CBL COACHING

BOOK 2
PHONICS AND LIFE SKILLS READING
FOR
Adult Literacy, ABE, and ESL Students
Turning Learners into Proficient Readers
CBL COACHING

BOOK 3
PHONICS AND LIFE SKILLS READING
FOR
Adult Literacy, ABE, and ESL Students
Turning Learners into Proficient Readers
CBL COACHING

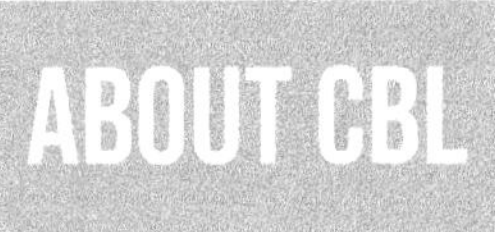

CBL equips programs and instructors to increase student retention, learning—and success.

We do it by offering evidence-based systematic solutions, learner-centered teaching materials, instructor-centered training, and future-oriented strategies in adult education, workforce development, and vocational training.

We teach proven insights, knowledge, and skills that are useful to practitioners (instructors, administrators, and support staff).

CBL also takes pride in publishing student-centered textbooks designed to prepare learners for CASAS, TABE, HiSET, and GED assessments and assist instructors in covering course curricula and standards with confidence.

Our publications also include teaching guides, test prep tools, and study guides that foster reflective learning, ensuring sustained engagement in active learning. Find our meticulously crafted textbooks on our book page (cbledu.com) or major platforms like Amazon, Barnes & Noble, and Ingram Spark.

CBL also guides adult education and workforce programs in establishing robust professional development programs—training, peer-mentoring, coaching, community of practices (CoPs), and instructional systems— fostering a culture of continuous improvement and contributing to higher learner retention and success rates. We also offer workshops and PD sessions for adult educators and classroom instructors.

If you have suggestions or questions about instructional systems, textbooks, or student learning and retention, contact us today at teamcbl@cbledu.com or 410-960-4082.

www.ingramcontent.com/pod-product-compliance
Lightning Source LLC
Chambersburg PA
CBHW081203130726
47996CB00009B/3228